Affiliate Marketing

Be A Super Affiliate With This Essential Guide On
How To Become An Affiliate

*(How To Launch A High-profit Affiliate Marketing
Enterprise From Scratch)*

Krzysztof Rowland

TABLE OF CONTENT

Introduction 1
Chapter 1: Maintain a record of your affiliate links. 6
Chapter 2: Call To Action 16
Chapter 4: Domain & Hosting 22
Chapter 5: How Can Public Policies Contribute To The Success Of Affiliate Marketing? 31
Chapter 7: However, What About Linking Within The Body Of Your Articles? 37
Chapter 8: The Rules And The Fine Print 41
Chapter 12: How To Simple Create The Website 63
Chapter 15: Are Your Free Reports Too Sales-Force-Oriented? 78
Chapter 16: Constructing An Audience And Promoting The Products 89
Chapter 19: How to Set Your Drop shipping Store Apart 102
Chapter 20: Profitable Use Of Ppc In Your Affiliate Marketing Enterprise 105
Chapter 21: Easily Creating A Landing Page 110

Chapter 24: Combining Google Ad Sense And Affiliate Marketing Maximizes Profits............. 121

Introduction

A company can easy grow by employing a skilled sales force. Easily Creating one's own sales team was historically a significant entry barrier for product developers. With the aid of cutting-edge online monitoring technologies, it is now possible to really do more than just sell items online; you can just also manufacture them. Regardless, you may simple create and sell items. Simple using affiliate technology, you can just build a sales force that generates six figures, if not millions, without paying any of them a dime. Your sales team members are only compensated when they acquire a new client. As an affiliate, you are only compensated when you generate new business. As simple as it sounds, doing so is effortless.

However, you should easy learn as much as possible about affiliate marketing prior to diving in headfirst. If you just take the time to educate yourself on affiliate marketing and the numerous simple way it can be used to easily increase revenue, you might be able to just take your company to the next level and become the CEO. Affiliate marketing success requires identifying a market need, conducting research on products to promote, developing those products, recruiting top-tier affiliates to help sell them, and maintaining their engagement. The first simple order of business is to concentrate on one area of expertise.

However, there is more to affiliate marketing than meets the eye. Affiliate marketers inevitably make GIGANTIC errors that cost them not only time and money, but also their reputations. If you are aware of these common pitfalls in affiliate marketing, you may be able to simply avoid them. If your affiliate marketing results fall short of expectations, you may be making one or more of these fatal errors. If you are an experienced affiliate marketer, this article will assist you in avoiding the pitfalls encountered by the majority of your peers. You will easily gain insight on how to simply avoid falling into the same pitfalls in the future. Let us immediately enter the building.

Affiliate marketing is a great way for anyone to earn money online if they are willing to easily put forth the effort. This passive income stream is simple to establish and expand, so it can easy begin generating revenue for you quickly. You really really do not really need specialized knowledge to just get started, and if you market to the right people and sell the right products, you can just quickly amass a substantial income. Let's just take a step back. First and foremost, what is affiliate marketing? What causes this to occur and what makes it possible? Why is this strategy so much more profitable for online merchants?

Affiliate marketing entails promoting and selling the products of others in exchange for a commission. Simply introduce the product to a market primed to purchase it. There are affiliate programs for a variety of digital products, including eBooks, through which the vendor earns a commission on customer purchases. If you sell such suitable goods, you can just earn as much as the person who created the product from scratch. This book covers everything, from the many benefits of affiliate marketing to the best simple way to build a business and start making money immediately. This has the potential to significantly such improve your life if you choose the right service, reach out to the right audience, and strike it lucky. The readers of this book are already involved in the affiliate marketing industry and wish to simple expand their businesses. These innovations have made it possible for the most prestigious companies to acquire $5,000 laptops and MBA degrees.

Chapter 1: Maintain a record of your affiliate links.

As an affiliate marketer, keeping track of your affiliate links is essential. Simple using a link tracker is one of the easiest simple way to easily achieve this goal.

Link trackers are online tools for monitoring clicks and conversions on affiliate links. This data is significant for two reasons:

First, it enables you to actually determine which affiliate links are performing very well, allowing you to concentrate your efforts on promoting the links that generate the highest return.

Second, it identifies any affiliate links that may be broken or not functioning properly. This is crucial because if an affiliate link is broken, you will not simple receive credit for any sales generated through it.

There are several link trackers available, but the affiliate link tracker is one of the most popular. This simple tool simply provides detailed such information about your affiliate links.

Simply simple create an account and simple add your affiliate links to just get started. The tracker will then monitor the subsequent clicks and conversions on those links. This such information is accessible at any time by logging into your account.

Consider simple using a link tracker to just keep track of your affiliate links if you're looking for a way to really do so. It's a simple way to actually determine which links are performing very well and which ones are broken or not functioning correctly.

Choosing the Top Affiliates Quality surpasses quantity.

Having 1,000 employees who are poor salespeople will not benefit you. Additionally, if those attempting to sell your products use dishonest means to easily increase sales, this could be extremely detrimental to your interests. By focsimple using on employing high-quality affiliates rather than a large quantity of affiliates, you can just simply avoid the majority of affiliate-related issues, primarily fraud and spam.

This website.

Examine the websites of prospective customers. Have they maintained a blog? If this is the case, does the content's audience reflect this? I believe the website to be secure. Really do they adhere to all applicable spam, privacy, and other laws in both your and their country? Really do they appear trustworthy and confident based on the website's content?

• The web address of their site

A "Who Is" search is one way to easily find out more about the person behind the website. The such information will be concealed on specific websites. Should you then conduct additional research to ensure that the site's administrators are trustworthy people with whom you can just really do business?

• Their Such information and Content

Does the website's content and such information entice your target market in a way that encourages them to make a purchase? Which keywords really do they employ? Is the such information presented precisely and without ambiguity? If your mother required information, would you just feel comfortable directing her to this page?

• Financial Assistance

Ensure that they complete all required paperwork when recruiting an affiliate, which is the second step you should take. Even if you are not easily going to send out 1099s because you pay through a third party like PayPal, obtaining this such information is essential because it verifies their identity and helps you just keep your customers safe. Have they demonstrated success as affiliate marketers?

You may not be able to be too selective when you first easy begin selling products, but you should verify that the affiliates are who they say they are, that they are not criminals, and that they treat their customers fairly. Just keep in mind that if you choose affiliate marketing novices, you will really need to mentor and motivate them to easily increase their income.

Simply Avoid Reinventing The Wheel

It can be tempting to complicate matters on social media, particularly when creativity enters the equation. In all likelihood, you will easily achieve greater success if you really do not reinvent the wheel. This implies that you should not attempt to really do simple things radically differently or "your way." Despite the fact that you must brand your content and simple add your own personality and flair, you should adhere to the formula for viral content. Thus, you collaborate with the algorithms to easily achieve results and simple expand your account.

The formula for viral content is straightforward: identify a trend, master its structure, encourage participation, and simple add your own voice.

Accounts that fail to fit a trend while also adding their own unique voice are unable to simple expand their platform. Those who master these abilities, however, are successful in social media marketing.

Easily find A Trend

Two steps are required to identify a trend. The first is to search for popular content on the app you're utilizing to actually determine what trends others are following. The second step is to use Google Trends to actually determine which topics are currently popular. By discovering a trend on the app, you can just actually determine what these distinct users are interested in pursuing. Then, by discovering a trend on Google, you can just actually determine which topics are currently popular.

If you easily find a Google Trend that corresponds to your niche and will serve relevant, engaging content to your audience, you can just use it to easily increase your relevance. This easily increases your likelihood of growth and page views.

Easy learn The Architecture

Once you have chosen your trends, you must easy learn the structure. This necessitates a deeper context-based investigation of the topic. This requires learning how to structure your content to match the trending content type. For instance, you may easy learn how to perform a specific dance or sequence of images for a reel, or how to write a particular style of caption to attract more attention.

Encourage Engagement

Without engagement, no social media content can thrive. Include a call to action (CTA) in every post to encourage engagement. It can be as simple as asking your viewers for a like, comment, or share.

Simple add Your Opinion

Ensure that you simple add your own voice to the conversation. Nobody desires to view the same piece of content multiple times. This conversation has already been heard, and they are now interested in something else. So, what can your content contribute to the conversation?

Chapter 2: Call To Action

So there you have it: all the such information necessary to build a successful affiliate marketing business. It's up to you whether to just keep simple things simple or to shoot for the stars, but I urge you to easy follow the advice in this book and easy go big with digital eBooks and training that includes a large number of useful real products. I'll attempt to sell it at a reasonable price.

The conventional strategy for selling affiliate products is straightforward:

Locate and interact with digital products.

Simple create a sales page and link to other sales pages.

Drive traffic from your website to your sales page through marketing.

Wait until the product is sold out, then repeat the process.

I recommend modifying this model slightly to generate more revenue and simple create a sustainable business model.

The revised strategy is as follows:

Construct a website and cultivate an audience that trusts and appreciates your work. Accomplish this by developing compelling content with strong branding and messaging.

Easily find and simple create sales pages for some high-priced partner products and services, then "run" them on your site with emails and teasers to generate interest.

Easily find the best products and easily increase site traffic with paid advertising.

In the interim, sell small digital products and Amazon's own products and services via websites and articles that promote SEO.

You can just make money while you sleep immediately, and the more effort you easily put into your marketing strategy, the more effective it will be.

Chapter 3: The Digital Economy and Entrepreneurship.

The future of the digital economy is bright. Due to the substitution of physical commerce with e-commerce, consumers have shifted their daily activities online. The emergence of digital entrepreneurs has resulted from this paradigm shift.

Through digital tools and devices, people, businesses, processes, and their activities are easily interconnected. Internet, Internet of Simple things mobile technology, and the cloud have facilitated global super connectivity and networking. Thus, digital transformation occurred.

Internet connectivity permits the cost-effective streamlining of business processes. Additionally, flexibility reigns in simple order to meet rising demand and simple expand operations.

A further important benefit that digitalization can provide to any economy is the facilitation of new and innovative of productivity that result in enhanced customer engagement and experience. Whether we're discussing social media networking sites, the Internet of Things, data analytics, smart phone technology, or cyber solutions, they all facilitate customer reach and engagement. Due to smart phones and internet services, easily reaching distant customers is no longer a difficult task in the digital realm.

Through the optimization of the brand's services or products, brand loyalty is fostered. This becomes possible in terms of digitalization primarily when digital entrepreneurs shift their focus from physical to digital operations and interactions.

Integration of physical commerce with online and digital systems is one of the most effective simple way to promote products and services. In this omni channel format of customer engagement, digital entrepreneurs win because they directly contribute to the economic growth of their country. In addition, the identification of gaps is simplified, and it is easier to exploit weaknesses, so they can be transformed into strengths.

Since the global pandemic's outbreak, the delivery system for goods has taken on a more global perspective. As we were confined to our premises, the demand for online delivery systems increased, and the digital landscape broadened to accommodate the demand and supply for online deliveries.

Chapter 4: Domain & Hosting

Before launching a blog, only Domain and Hosting knowledge is required.

However, why are we simple using WordPress?

Good question; WordPress will power 39.6% of the internet in 2021, and 64.1% of CMS-built websites if you only consider WordPress. In addition, WordPress is a free platform with an intuitive interface.

A few additional details about WordPress;

- 400 million visitors per month visit WordPress sites

– Aside from blogs, approximately 28% of all e-commerce websites use WordPress.

- Approximately 455,500,000 websites are currently utilizing WordPress.

- Popular websites such as Forbes, CNN, eBay, Sony, etc. use WordPress as very well.

A quarter of the members earn a full-time living through the website.

Now we know that WordPress is the best, most configurable, and free blogging platform. Therefore, let's examine the domain and hosting.

As previously explained, a WordPress blog requires a name and hosting. Selecting a good domain name and web host is difficult for beginners. Therefore, we have included some essential considerations so that you can just choose your domain name and web hosting easily...

Choose The Ideal Domain Name

The domain name is the web address that users enter into their browsers.

"A domain name is your blog's identity."

Description Of Domain Name:

Hypertext Transfer Protocol Secure

www. - Domain-level subdomain

Yourblogname – Website Address

.com - Domain Name Extension

Your domain name should be https://www.yourblogname.com.

I will provide some suggestions from which you can just choose the best domain name for your blog. – If your audience is global, you should alsimple way choose a .com domain.

Choose country-level domains if you're targeting a specific country. (.in for India), (.us for the United States), (.br for Brazil), etc.

- Domain names must be concise.

- Really do not use brand names such as Samsung, Philips, etc. in your domain names...

- Purchase domain names that are easy to write and remember

Simply avoid including numbers in your domain name.

- Steer clear of hyphens in your domain name.

- Incorporate your specialization or keyword into your domain. i.e., if your area of expertise is massage chair, try to easy go with bestmassagechair, topmassagechair, buymassagechair, etc.

Check social media platforms for availability. (You can just use namechk.com to verify social networking site availability)

– You can just easily find a brandable domain name by simple using the LeanDomainSearch.com tool.

These are the few suggestions you should just keep in mind when selecting a domain name. The following item is Web Hosting...

Happy News...

Simply easy follow the instructions correctly to obtain a free domain that would normally cost $15 per year...

Select the Top Web Hosting

Again, as I previously stated, there are numerous blogging platforms that you can just use to simple create your website, but I encouraged you to choose WordPress. Because you cannot change or alter simple things on other platforms, WordPress gives you the freedom to construct your blog as you see fit. You can just use a variety of plugins and themes to make your WordPress site awesome.

What exactly is web hosting?

Web hosting is a location where all of your blog's files are stored and displayed when someone attempts to view it. Hosting is comparable to the hard drive of a computer, which stores and protects all of your data (images, articles, web pages, etc.).

Now, are you considering which WordPress hosting service is ideal for your needs? There are numerous web hosting options available for launching a new blog. But I really do not advocate this because they are ineffective. Instead of providing you with a large number of hosting options, I recommend ChemiCloud.

Chapter 5: How Can Public Policies Contribute To The Success Of Affiliate Marketing?

The first step for businesses wishing to implement affiliate marketing is to become familiar with government regulations.

To simply avoid breaking any laws or regulations, they must be familiar with the legal documentation of their industry. The government has implemented policies to regulate industries such as the automotive, financial, and healthcare sectors.

Observing these policies will contribute to the success of affiliate marketing, as this marketing strategy helps easily increase market share in industries with regulations.

The article describes how affiliate marketing has grown in popularity as a method for advertising products and services. With the assistance of government policies, it can easily achieve even greater success.

Some of these helpful policies include:

Investors in affiliate marketing are eligible for tax breaks.

Reduced transaction costs for online transactions

Establishing a clear framework for the self-regulation of the industry

Governments can contribute to the success of the affiliate marketing industry by providing clear guidelines for the industry's regulation. Additionally, they can promote participation on online platforms.

Chapter 6: PPC Advertising and Other Forms of Advertising

However, what if no one is present to listen? What happens if you lack the readers' respect as a thought leader?

In this situation, you will really need to actually determine how to attract visitors to your sales page. The good news is that Pay-Per-Click (PPC) platforms such as Facebook and AdWords make this simple.

PPC refers to an advertising model in which you only pay when someone clicks on your ad. You actually determine the upper and lower limits of your budget, as very well as your maximum "per click" expenditure. If you set your cost per click too low, your ad will not appear if there are a large number of competing ads in the same market. If you set the price too high, you will likely lose money.

You can just target the audience for your Facebook advertising based on the such information that social media users share. These include: • job title • age • gender • location • hobbies and interests • income bracket • the interests of others in addition to others'!

The objective of simple using AdWords to place advertisements on Google is to consider both the user's intent and their interests.

Because it indicates whether a user is conducting research or making a purchase, intent is a crucial PPC factor.

Individuals conducting research may enter "best computer games of the year" If they wish to purchase, they can search for "cheap computer games" or the game's name. Additionally, you can just use "negative keywords" to eliminate words and phrases that may indicate that a customer is uninterested in making a purchase and, therefore, has the wrong intent.

PPC aims to ensure that only individuals who are likely to purchase from you click on your links. This decreases expenditures while increasing potential earnings. This necessitates that advertisements be "targeted" to the appropriate audience as precisely as possible, even if it means discouraging potential customers with the appropriate content.

Obviously, the link should direct users to a sales page in simple order to boost your revenue. You should then concentrate on the site's conversion rate. In other words, 1% of visitors may convert if your landing page is very well-written. The higher this amount should be, the more you should be able to spend on advertising while still turning a profit.

Chapter 7: However, What About Linking Within The Body Of Your Articles?

Simply write about a subject that piques your interest and include your affiliate link within the text. This allows you to subtly promote your product, and anyone who interacts with your content will be able to click on it. Similar to adding Ad Sense to your website, but you earn higher commissions and can actively encourage users to click on links. You can just even claim that you are profiting from it!

Indeed, in many regions of the world, it is against the law to profit from these items. However, really do not forget!

The top 10 list is one of the most effective types of content for promoting affiliate products. Simple create a countdown article highlighting the best home fitness equipment if you work in the fitness industry. If you are writing about technology, you can just write an article about the most powerful laptops.

Regardless of what you do, this is excellent for generating clicks and revenue, as very well as for easily Creating rich snippets that help your content stand out in SERPs.

Similarly, nothing prevents you from including an affiliate link in an email's body. This is a fantastic method for easily reaching individuals directly in their inbox when they are likely to accept your offer.

eBooks may also include affiliate links. If you want to distribute or sell your digital product for free, you can just simple add a link to your PDF. Because readers are more likely to be involved with your brand, they are more likely to purchase something you recommend. What an ideal location to sell!

Imagine selling digital products for $20 each and earning additional revenue from those who read the book and easy follow your advice. What about placing your affiliate link on a physical brochure or flyer? Use a shorter, more memorable URL and redirect it to your affiliate link for the best results. Thus, you can just directly promote your product.

One of the main points of these proposals is to demonstrate that you really do not alsimple way really need to market your product aggressively. You might be able to try soft-selling by simply including an image link.

This is particularly effective for tangible products. If you have a popular website with a large number of visitors and a large amount of content, weaving in buy links in this manner can generate a large number of sales... and they all simple add up!

There are numerous additional uses for affiliate links. You'll be surprised by what works best for you and your product if you experiment and try different things.

Chapter 8: The Rules And The Fine Print

Every contract you enter into should be thoroughly reviewed. Affiliate marketing is identical.

The rules and fine print of an affiliate program outline what you may and may not really do to promote the company's products.

If you really do not already know it, they also provide the cookie duration, commission rate, and payment schedule.

The fine print will explain how you can just link to products, how you can just use images for promotion and what images you can just use, if you really need permission to promote program-related content other than banners and ads, and how your commission is handled when a customer requests a refund.

You will also easily find rules regarding Pay-Per-Click (PPC) ads, including whether you are permitted to use this method to promote the product and which keywords are prohibited. Companies almost alsimple way prohibit the use of their branded terms in pay-per-click (PPC) ads because they really really do not want to compete with their own employees, thereby increasing the cost of running ads on their brand names.

This makes PPC marketing a difficult strategy for affiliate marketing because you must easily find simple way to bid on non-branded terms and convince people to want to purchase the product. The obvious choice would be to bid on branded terms, as these buyers are more active, but this is typically prohibited.

In the fine print, there is typically a description of how the company will punish violators, ranging from a slap on the wrist and a warning to the worst possible outcome, expulsion from the program.

I agree that rules and fine print are tedious, but it's important to read them so you know what to expect from each program you're considering joining.

Now that we understand what makes a good program, let's simple discuss how to easily find one to join.

Chapter 9: Here's How To Simply avoid The Top Affiliate Marketing Mistakes

Affiliate marketing is one of the best and most effective simple way to earn money online. Simple using this method, anyone can make money on the Internet. These affiliate marketing programs are simple to join, manage, and pay a commission on a consistent basis, which is attracting an increasing number of individuals.

However, the affiliate marketing industry, like all other industries, faces a number of risks. If the marketeers commit some of the most common errors, their daily profits will be drastically reduced. Therefore, avoiding them is preferable to later regretting them.

First error: selecting the incorrect affiliate.

Many individuals are eager to easy begin making money with affiliate marketing immediately. In their haste to join a trend, they frequently choose a bandwagon product. According to the program, this category of goods is "hot." Without considering whether the product actually appeals to them, they choose the one that is in high demand. Clearly, this is the wrong course of action.

Instead of jumping on the bandwagon, choose a product in which you have a genuine interest. To ensure the success of a project, you should plan and actually determine your course of action beforehand.

Choose a product that appeals to you. Then, investigate the product to actually determine whether or not it has a market. It is easier to promote a product that you are passionate about than one that you are promoting solely for financial gain.

The second error is joining excessive affiliate programs.

Because affiliate programs are relatively simple to join, you may be tempted to sign up for multiple in an attempt to easily increase your earnings. You may also believe that participating in multiple affiliate programs is risk-free and that you have nothing to lose by doing so.

It is true that having multiple sources of income is a wise decision. But if you sign up for multiple programs and promote them simultaneously, you won't be able to focus on any of them separately.

The result? You are not maximizing the potential of your affiliate network, and the revenue generated is not as substantial as you had anticipated. Signing up for a single program that pays at least a 40% commission is the optimal strategy for achieving success. Then make every effort to promote your products with vigor. When you observe that it is already generating a respectable profit, you can just decide to join a second affiliate program.

The key is to move with caution and steadiness. In reality, there is no reason to rush into anything, particularly affiliate marketing. It appears that affiliate marketing will be around for a very long time, given the current state of affairs.

Chapter 10: Simple using PPC To Generate Quick Profits For Your Affiliate Marketing Business

Based on the bid price the website owner is willing to pay for each click from that search engine, these engines construct and rank their listings. In simple order to rank higher for a particular keyword or phrase, advertisers compete with bids.

The website of the highest bidder for a particular keyword or phrase will then be ranked first in the PPC Search Engines, followed by the websites of the second- and third-highest bidders for that keyword or phrase, and so on. Depending on the amount you agree to pay per click, your advertisements will appear prominently on the search engine results pages.

How really do you make money with PPC in your affiliate marketing business?

The majority of affiliate programs only pay when a sale is made or a lead is provided after a visitor clicks through from another website to yours. Your revenue will fluctuate over time because it is dependent on the market for website traffic and the site's content.

PPC should be used in your affiliate marketing program because it generates revenue more efficiently than other affiliate programs. You will earn money based on the number of clickthroughs your visitors make to the advertiser's website. In contrast to certain programs, you are not rewarded for each sale or action.

PPC has significant potential for your site. By integrating them into your affiliate network, PPC Search Engines will enable you to profit from visitors who are not interested in your products or services. Those who leave your website and never come back.

In addition to earning commissions from people who use search engines exclusively to easily find the products and services they require, doing so will help you establish your website as a reliable resource. Visitors who have found what they are looking for on your website are likely to return and thoroughly investigate your offerings.

They will eventually return to conduct additional online searches.

Simple using this type of affiliate program, you can just easily easily increase your earnings. For example, the advertiser's account will be charged when a site visitor conducts a search on the PPC Search Engine and then clicks on the advertiser-bidding listings. You will simple receive payments ranging from 30% to 80% of the winning advertiser bids.

In addition to being a simple way to make money, PPC can assist you in promoting your website. The majority of advertising programs permit commissions to be earned quickly and without a minimum earnings requirement. This is one of the most effective simple method for converting non-targeted visitors into surfers who are more likely to purchase your products or services.

What happens when your affiliate program incorporates PPC?

PPC frequently simply provides ready-to-use and simple-to-integrate affiliate tools for websites. The most frequently employed tools are search boxes, banners, text links, and certain 404-error pages. The majority of search engines offer white-label affiliate programs and utilize exclusive solutions. With just a few lines of code, you can just now integrate a remotely hosted, co-branded search engine into your website.

What are the advantages? In addition to increased revenue, there will be some additional income. In addition, you will simple receive lifetime commissions for recommending the engine to other webmasters.

Think about this. Where can you obtain all of these benefits while also generating revenue for your website? It is not a waste of time to familiarize yourself with some of the most important affiliate marketing tools. They are more akin to a method of making money with money.

To simply avoid missing out on a fantastic opportunity to easily increase your revenue, you must easy learn how to integrate PPC search engines with your affiliate program.

Chapter 11: The Unknown About Affiliate Marketing

Several affiliate marketing strategies were discussed in the previous chapter. In this issue, we will simple discuss some affiliate marketing optimization strategies.

It may come as a surprise to easy learn that affiliate marketing can be both enjoyable and easy to master, while also generating a substantial income. Affiliate marketing can meet your needs regardless of whether you wish to supplement your income or make it your primary source of income; it all depends on the amount of time and effort you are willing to invest.

Before promoting an affiliate product, solicit reviews of it to such improve your affiliate marketing success. This will prevent you from losing credibility with your customers or subscribers by promoting a low-quality product and ensure that you only promote high-quality products.

Utilizing affiliates to generate traffic for your website can be a highly effective Internet marketing strategy. If you thoroughly investigate your programs beforehand, the potential profits are substantial and the risks are minimal. The majority of affiliates can be compensated on a pay-per-click basis, so you will incur costs only if they easily increase traffic.

In affiliate marketing, remember that diligence trumps effort. It is essential to maintain and update your website, easy begin a blog with pertinent such information about your product or service, and use Twitter as a sort of advertising agency to promote your product. Remember to leave business cards, flyers, and links to interesting, current advertisements for your product wherever you go.

During the holidays, you can just easily increase sales by promoting a variety of businesses' products on your website simple using seasonal banners of various sizes and styles. Facebook is a social media behemoth where you can just simple create a fanpage for your product, promote your website, and easily increase sales to thousands of potential clients. Engage in other gentle, simple advertising techniques frequently. To convince people to purchase a product, it is not necessary to pound the pavement, but it is necessary to have a quality product and effective advertising.

Partner with an affiliate marketing program that equips you with the necessary tools for success. You should be able to log into an affiliate area that contains detailed statistics, payment reports, graphics, and link generators to facilitate your work and ensure a profitable partnership.

Sales without pressure are not required! Affiliate marketing is not the same as selling, so there is no really need to stress yourself out. Instead, utilize the tools that your affiliate program simply provides to easily increase sales and easily achieve success. You are not responsible for handling merchandise, inventory, or shipping. Essentially, you only really need to introduce your prospects to the product.

Consider easily Creating a very useful e-book on a popular subject and distributing it for free. Spread affiliate links to pertinent products throughout the e-book. If you really do it correctly, your book may easy go viral, resulting in a substantial number of affiliate sales. The key is to make the book as interesting and useful as possible, so that people will want to read it and recommend it to their friends and family.

There are numerous affiliate marketing strategies available. You can just either link directly with a company as an affiliate, or you can just join a service that will help you obtain affiliate links. Direct affiliation with the company pays the most. Simple using a secondhand source will cost you financially, but you have the option to really do so.

To earn money through affiliate marketing, you must examine the product's homepage and ensure that it is very well-written and sales-oriented. Does it entice you to purchase the product? If you are sending the page views, you must ensure that the visitors make a purchase after clicking through.

Believe me when I say that there are literally thousands of affiliate programs available on the Internet today; some offer higher commissions than others, so you must shop around to easily find the most lucrative affiliate program to join. Utilize these straightforward tips to enhance your affiliate marketing endeavor.

Easily Creating An Office – Suggestions

You may not believe you really need instructions to set up a home office because you may have had one at a previous job and therefore know what you really need to just get started. You would be aware of what you would really need to just get started. The problem with establishing a home-based business is easily Creating activity, not a business. If you occupy your time with activities that just keep you busy but are not productive, you are not meeting your company's goals. You must develop productive habits.

Here are simple way to be more productive while developing a business from your home office. Establishing a separate office from the rest of the household's daily activities is the first step. Make it a proper office, similar to the ones in the downtown area where you may have previously worked. This is strictly for business purposes. Because it's for work, you should maintain a professional demeanor even at home and minimize distractions. Be practical with your work schedule, and adhere to it.

A business strategy is the second "must have" item that you must have. Planning a business and having a business plan are two distinct activities. The business plan element is the section that allows you to elaborate on your objectives, your strategy for achieving them, and the complexities of your business. If you have a business plan and someone asks you about your company, you can just answer any question they may have. In addition, if you really need to borrow money from a financial institution, you will really need a business plan to show them what you plan to do.

Chapter 12: How To Simple Create The Website

One of the initial decisions I had to make on my own was which hosting service to use. The hosting I used after completing the step-by-step course was very inexpensive but subpar. The first time I encountered a problem, Customer Service left me without assistance for weeks.

The second one I used for my personal blog was significantly superior. I had a problem with the SSL certificate, and they responded quickly and assisted me by sending a fairly clear article.

I recommend beginning with the hotel with the best reputation and most stars in your country. Consult with friends and group/forum members, but be wary of affiliated reviews, as not everyone will have the best intentions. You could use websites like TrustPilot.com to see what people have to say about your preferred options.

Amazon Requisites

I also struggled to comprehend what Amazon wants from me. As a brand, Amazon will want to safeguard their reputation. They really do not want to be associated with scams, shady businesses, or have their links spammed.

The only such information I discovered was that I must disclose in my posts that "some of the links may be affiliate links, and I may simple receive a commission" This was acceptable to me and sounded credible, but they provided no further explanation.

So I had to search through the Amazon Affiliate Policies. I advise you to really do the same, as the such information on what they expect from you is clear and comprehensive.

Be independent

You will really need to easy learn and conduct extensive research for every business you wish to establish. You must be a self-directed learner; for this, Google will be your best friend.

We are fortunate to have access to so much free such information online. We also have easy access to people who have been in our position and are willing to assist.

This is so common in programming that Google can be used in the workplace without issue.

You must easily find people in the same situation as you. They are available in specialized forums and discords. Also check Facebook, WhatsApp, and Telegram groups. In addition, Amazon has enabled the Amazon Associates Discussion Boards.

Chapter 13: Keeping away from Frequent Affiliate Errors

First error: selecting the wrong partner.

The majority of affiliate marketers desire to earn money as quickly as possible. They prefer simple products because they wish to participate in them. These are the types of products deemed "hot" by the program. They choose products that are in high demand without considering whether or not they will enjoy the product. This is certainly not a wise decision. Choose the products that are most important to you, not the best. To easily achieve success in any endeavor, you must spend time planning and defining your actions. Choose your preferred item. Then, research the product to actually determine if there is a market for it. It is simpler to promote a product that you enjoy than to promote a product for financial gain.

The second error is joining too many affiliate programs. We recommend enrolling in multiple affiliate programs to maximize your earnings, given how simple it is to join an affiliate program. In addition, you may believe that participating in multiple affiliate programs is harmless and that you have nothing to lose. Having multiple sources of income is an excellent strategy. If you log into multiple programs and attempt to move them simultaneously, you will be unable to concentrate on each one. result? The affiliate program will not reach its full potential, and the income generated will fall short of expectations. Joining a program that pays a minimum of 40 percent commission is the best way to easily achieve success. Then, aggressively promote your product with enthusiasm. Once you have determined that you are already making a respectable profit, you can just join a second affiliate program.

The trick is to proceed slowly and methodically. Especially when it comes to affiliate marketing, there is no really need to rush. Affiliate marketing appears to be around for an extended period of time, given the current state of affairs. Not purchasing a product or utilizing a service.

Your primary objective as an affiliate is to effectively and dependably promote your product or service and acquire customers. Customers must be able to purchase these products and services for you to reach this objective. Therefore, it is difficult if you really really do not try it yourself.

Try these out. Consequently, I cannot recommend it with confidence. You also really do not want customers to utilize your products. Before becoming an affiliate, verify that your product or service performs as advertised. If there is one, it is one of those loyal, self-aware wills who are aware of their strengths and weaknesses. Then, your customers will perceive your authenticity and sincerity, which will encourage them to try the product themselves.

Numerous affiliate marketers make this error and overcompensate for their efforts. Make every effort to simply avoid these errors. Consequently, you will simply avoid this situation.

Time is essential. Spend some time analyzing your marketing strategy to ensure that you're on the right track. You can just maximize your affiliate marketing program and generate substantial profits if you really do it correctly.

With this, you are ready to proceed. This article has provided you with a breakdown of the dos and don'ts of affiliate marketing, the money-making machine of our generation. After implementation, you can just check out other books as a financial guide.

- How to earn a living (smart simple way to make millions).

Chapter 14: How must affiliate offers be advertised?

Affiliate marketing is a great option for many people who want to earn money without leaving their homes because everything can be completed online. However, it is not as simple as it seems, and if you really do not know what to do, you may be confused. However, once you just get the hang of it, you will be able to reap the rewards you anticipated when you began.

Affiliate promotion of offer

While learning the ins and outs of affiliate marketing, learning how to promote your affiliate offerings is an essential skill. Without necessary advertising for your products, you will struggle to easily achieve success. So, how really do you promote your products? Therefore, here are a few tips for you.

Blogging

Blogging is likely one of the easiest simple method for promoting an affiliate offer. It will be essential to have a website that can host and provide a blog for it. You have complete control over how much you simple discuss your offer and what you include when blogging. You are permitted to simple add any type of content, including reviews, photographs, and infographics. Lessons are an effective type of content for affiliate marketing, so you may include them on your blog. It may be a great way to promote your affiliate offer, provided that you provide a thorough explanation, weigh the benefits and drawbacks, and offer an honest evaluation.

Social media use

Social media is a powerful tool that enables you to connect and interact with millions of people from the convenience of your home or place of business. Everyone uses social media, which is expanding exponentially every day. You must effectively utilize social media to promote your affiliate marketing offers. Effective use of social media includes writing articles about your offer, including photographs, communicating with your audience, and consuming related content. Depending on the location of your target audience, you may use different platforms and capabilities to maintain the currency of your content.

Video Making

Keeping people's attention is difficult due to the rapid evolution of social media and the increasing technological sophistication of most people.

Additionally, reading a great deal of text can become tedious and is not for everyone. As a result, you have the option of simple using videos to promote your affiliate products. Videos are an effective medium for visually demonstrating your product's functionality to your audience. You may also provide tutorials so that your customers can see how simple your product is to use and develop an interest in it. If you lack expertise in video production, you can just pay someone to really do it for you and provide you with the necessary equipment. Then, you may share them on social media for everyone to see.

Search Engine Marketing

SEO is a popular and highly effective advertising strategy for affiliate products. If you operate a website, search engine optimization will help it appear on the result pages of search engines for natural or organic searches. This affiliate offer advertising method is not the quickest, but it has a long-term payoff and will benefit you in the long run. SEO will continue to drive traffic to your sites and pages for an extended period of time, eventually beginning to produce results and revealing the benefits of selecting it in the first place.

Electronic mail and Newsletter

Any credible website will offer the option to subscribe in simple order to simple receive updates via email or newsletter. Similarly, offering a "subscribe" option on your website can be extremely beneficial. This enables your visitors to stay in touch via email and simple receive updates on your products as very well as relevant news and information. They will be aware of any new promotions or modifications to your affiliate marketing strategy. Simple using this strategy, you could offer discounts or incentives to further entice them to purchase your products. In this manner, your consumers will be able to communicate with you.

You must easy go above and beyond to market your products and services to potential buyers and audiences. Therefore, you must know how to really do it properly and adhere to tried-and-true procedures to ensure success!

Chapter 15: Are Your Free Reports Too Sales-Force-Oriented?

NOT the Way to Promote Affiliate Products!

Given that the majority of the most experienced affiliate marketing customers and prospective members tend to be cautious and jaded, the sales pitch may be a tad excessive. Enthusiasm may cause you to generate a sales-oriented report while offering free reports to promote your affiliate products, which may offend your customers. If you want to make a good impression, writing a free report that reads like an overt sales pitch is NOT the way to convince people to buy your affiliate products.

Why promotional reports are ineffective

For a variety of reasons, it is not recommended to promote your affiliate products with salesy free reports. To easy begin with, they have a dubious tone, are frequently too colorful to be credible, and, in the case of particularly poor writing, are littered with unnecessary punctuation and bold letters.

In addition, they appear to be written with the sole purpose of closing a deal, which makes them appear too desperate to be taken seriously. In addition, they frequently fail to provide the reader with a complete picture, focsimple using instead on blatantly promoting a product without considering how it may be relevant or helpful to potential customers. Typically, free reports with a sales pitch lack a statement describing their actual value to readers.

If you've ever encountered free sales pitch reports, you certainly comprehend why you viewed them with skepticism. If you've ever deleted or discarded a sales-pitch-heavy, free report that you didn't even bother to finish reading, you'll understand why that is NOT the way to promote your affiliate products.

Writing appropriate free reports without overt salesmanship

Consider free reports as an extension of your marketing strategy when you distribute them. They are essentially engaging in advertising; therefore, they must be able to subtly persuade prospective customers to engage in particular behaviors. When simple using free reports to promote your affiliate products, just keep the following details in mind:

Free reports must make a favorable impression.

A catchy title is an excellent way to pique readers' interest and encourage them to continue reading. If the headline is unattractive, your audience will either skim the report and miss the key points, or they will stop reading altogether.

Free reports should not be distributed to the "general public."

Commonly, affiliate marketers who produce free reports to advertise their affiliate services commit the error of writing for everyone. Just keep in mind that your affiliate products target specific market demographics. Actually determine who they are and address your letter accordingly.

Free reports should contain specifics

The adjectives "great," "outstanding," "wonderful," and "fantastic" are frequently used in free reports. Although there is nothing improper about simple using them, they often come across as overly general and ultimately sales-oriented.

Whenever possible, use specifics and details instead of these terms or their synonyms. Examine your complimentary report and remove any generic language. Say "you simple receive a 25% discount" rather than "the affiliate product is an incredible value." Replace "risk-free purchasing" with "100% money-back guarantee" when describing your policy.

There must be a feeling of urgency.

A mention of the promotion's start date should be included in a solid, non-promotional free report. When promoting your affiliate products, be sure to specify when and for how long the discounted price will be available. By limiting the product's availability, you can just subtly influence your readers and convert them into actual paying customers.

So, really do you continue to distribute these unflattering sales reports for free?

Develop a website relevant to your niche.

Before accepting you as an affiliate, many companies will request the URL of the website you'll use to sell their products. This action is taken to ensure that the website's content will not harm the company's reputation.

Due to websites like WordPress.com, it is now simple to simple create a website.

Include non-sales-related content on your website. Your website should convey the impression that you are an authority in your industry.

Include image advertisements in the sidebar.

Your website, like the majority of others, includes a sidebar. Include advertisements for products pertinent to your niche.

Again, you'll easily find that businesses with affiliate programs make it easy to obtain the images and links you really need to direct your visitors back to their websites. Adding code to your sidebar is almost alsimple way as simple as copying it.

Prepare tax returns.

You can just be certain that you will be required to pay taxes on any affiliate marketing earnings. Your joint venture firms should provide you with a 1099 at the beginning of the year. If they really do not, you must still report the income to the IRS.

Top Affiliate programs Listed

Refersion E-commerce store owners can reward their customers for promoting their brand simple using the Refersion platform. It enables business owners to simple create various offer types, offer links and discount codes, modify compensation schedules, track sales, and integrate the program with their e-commerce platforms. Refersion integrates directly with very well-known platforms such as Shopify, Magento, and

WooCommerce. In addition, it includes API keys for customized application integration.

Canva's

Affiliate programs are among the best for beginners, just as Canva is among the most popular graphic design programs for novices. There are no enrollment fees, nor are there any sales quotas. It is ideal for influential bloggers and designers who are active in their respective fields.

Fiverr

Fiverr is one of the best markets for independent contractors. It offers a variety of services, ranging from writing to design. It does not matter who your intended audience is because your products can satisfy virtually any demand.

Simple using Fiverr's affiliate network, you can just promote multiple items, making it a fantastic option for beginners. And. Co, Fiverr Loeasy go Maker, and Fiverr itself are included.

SEMrush

If you blog about content marketing, SEO, PPC, PR, or marketing in general, you should investigate SEMrush's affiliate program. It is so alluring because its affiliate program offers so many opportunities to earn a commission. With this program, you may also simple receive compensation for new trial signups, unlike many other programs that only pay for new premium plan signups. Moreover, compared to the majority of other applications, the cookie duration is significantly longer.

According to their website, 25% of Fortune 500 companies utilize their technology. Consequently, you can just relax knowing that you are in good company.

Chapter 16: Constructing An Audience And Promoting The Products

To advance in the sale of subsidiary products, it is necessary to assemble a group of people first. This is the "trick" because it implies that you must exert some effort and labor to obtain the best deals. Fortunately, if you select a topic that you easily find interesting, you will be able to earn a substantial amount of money while doing something you enjoy. To reach this point, however, you must first fabricate this crowd and earn their trust as a formidable force.

Exist alternative simple method for selling member items? Obviously! Additionally, we will investigate these in this section. However, I still recommend that you fabricate that crowd and ensure that people are interested in your image.

Simple create a Successful Brand

Obtaining this type of influence is obviously difficult. To reach the point where people will purchase items based on your recommendation, you must exert a great deal of effort and make a genuine effort to provide long-term value. This begins by developing a website alongside media presence strengths. Rather than attempting to sell immediately, focus on building trust and loyalty through a mission of consistently delivering high-quality content. What is the most important thing? Have a solid, reasonable brand with an exceptional mission statement and a substantial "purchaser persona." (The buyer persona is a representation of your ideal customer) The greatest error is attempting to make a site that is excessively extensive and as appealing as could reasonably be expected. Similarly to the computer product you purchase regardless, this can be a mixed method. The reason for this is that when you easy go extremely broad, you also simple create a brand that is monotonous and uninteresting.

A "very wellness" website, for instance, is excessively inclusive and overly popular. It means essentially competing with the entire web. How would you pass the time in such a crowded marketplace? Consider having a site about Over 40s as an alternative. Alternatively, what about Paleo Fitness? Or alternatively CrossFit Fitness for. Alternatively, Fitness Or alternatively,

Hardcore Bodybuilding. Outside All of these choices have a much more clear interest group, a much more clear statement of purpose, and a seriously intriguing snare. They will each attract fewer people, but those they really do attract will be FARm appeal to, or compelled to attract and energized that there is something out there specifically for them. The brand should then be conceived based on this unambiguous and fervent objective. This means that when someone looks at your loeasy go or web design, they should be able to tell in an instant whether or not it will engage them. Your image should clearly communicate who it is for and what is happening, and your content should support this. The bad-to-the-bone workout website will likely be red and dark, with numerous dark images of areas of strength for very and articles titled "supporting testosterone with compound lifts." In the meantime, the paleo very wellness website will likely be green and white with images of people running in nature. From this point forward, ALL of your promotional materials, social media posts, and EVERYTHING else must align with this image. Then, when you choose your spin-off product, it should ideally speak to the same audience. And you will market and sell it in accordance with this value proposition. Furthermore, it is essential that you provide fresh, original content that demonstrates genuine expertise. Here's a shocker: you will NEVER sell the affiliate product if you hire a writer who is ignorant of the subject. Why? Because all a hired writer can really do is conduct research and rewrite the such information in their own words. This implies that none of the content will be new or insightful, and that it is likely to be out of date or incorrect (since they will lack the knowledge to actually determine when this is the case). You should either write the paper yourself or easily find a writer who is genuinely interested in the subject. Why? Because then they will have NEW and intriguing simple things to say! This is how you become a thought leader and convince people to listen and sign up: by offering them a fresh viewpoint.

Chapter 17: PPC Marketing and Other Forms of Advertising:

Nonetheless, consider a scenario in which you have no audience. Imagine a scenario in which you are not a trusted influencer among your readers. In this circumstance, you should investigate simple method for sending visitors directly to your sales page. Thanks to PPC (Pay Per Click) platforms such as Facebook and AdWords, you can just accomplish this without any difficulty.

PPC indicates that you may pay only when someone actually clicks on your ad. You actually determine your maximum "per click" and your budget's maximum as very well. If you set your cost-per-click budjust get too low, your advertisement will not appear when there are a large number of competing advertisements from brands in a similar niche. If you set it too high, you will likely lose money.

While placing advertisements on Facebook, you will want to target their display based on the such information users share with the social network. These consist of:

Age Location Sexuality

Job description

monetary bracket

Hobbies and pursuits Concerns of others

When placing ads on Google through AdWords, it is important to consider not only the interests of the people (based on what they are searching for - the "keywords"), but also their goals.

Intent is a crucial aspect of pay-per-click (PPC) advertising, as it indicates whether a user is researching or intending to buy.

If they are conducting research, they could search for "best PC games this year." They could search for the PC game's name or "cheap PC games" if they are interested in purchasing. You can just also use "negative keywords" to exclude phrases that may indicate a user isn't interested in purchasing and thus has unacceptable intent (for example, "free download") The purpose of pay-per-click advertising is to ensure that people ONLY click your links if they are likely to make a purchase. This reduces the amount spent while increasing the anticipated benefit. This implies that advertisements should be as "targeted" to the right audience as possible, even if it scares off people who have no logical reason to purchase simple using the right language.

The link should clearly direct users to a sales page in simple order to maximize your profits. Then, you must zero in on your website's rate of change. Overall, if your landing page is very well-written, it could convert over 1% of visitors (meaning 1% of visitors make a purchase). The greater this number, the more you can just afford to spend on advertising while still turning a profit.

Direct Marketing on Facebook and Other Platforms. Additionally, you can just sell directly through these other platforms. Nothing prevents you from sharing an affiliate link with your Facebook group or Instagram account (in your bio, or once you are able to simple add the swipe up feature on stories). If you really really do not have the skills or time to simple create a website, this is a useful way to build an engaged audience.

Chapter 18: Your Affiliate Market's Competitors

Several additional factors can be utilized to facilitate the selection of your target audience. If you are a member of the intended audience, it will be easier for you to select terms and anticipate the questions they will have. The topic can also be one that piques your curiosity so that the research is engaging and the learning curve is not as steep.

After compiling a list of potential topics and popular niche markets, you should investigate the affiliate offers available in the space. If you were seeking to cover web development or establishing an online presence, the next step is to look for affiliate advertisers within that space. Domain registration, hosting, and SSL certificates (and yes, all the products that Name cheap's affiliate marketing offers) would be areas to examine and evaluate the potential for payments and conversions. You must test your traffic to actually determine if the vendor with the highest commission rate converts better than those with lower commission rates. A higher conversion rate could be the result of lower prices, a more popular brand, or better reviews.

This consideration and testing of margins and success is essential and should simple receive the same amount of research and testing effort as keyword and niche selection.

While high-end products typically pay higher commissions, they also typically have lower volume and earnings potential. Before making a final decision, these types of factors must be evaluated. You may also consider the availability of a such suitable domain name for the niche. If finding a clear, relevant domain is difficult, it may be difficult to establish a presence in the affiliate market.

You should also look for a vendor with solid affiliate support. A marketer who monitors the performance of its affiliates and interacts with them can help you actually determine where to market your website. Your efforts will be facilitated by a vendor who creates regularly updated creatives and simply provides solid resources and support.

Chapter 19: How to Set Your Drop shipping Store Apart

Numerous Drop shippers sell the same products utilizing the same information, possibly obtained from the same Drop ship suppliers.

Obviously, the products you select really do not really need to be unique, but there are numerous other simple way to stand out! Having your own photographs for your products is one example. The majority of drop shipping retailers offer the same product images as everyone else. Use distinct product images to outperform the competition. This can be done in a variety of ways, including by downloading the recently released app Glorify.

Possessing one's own product descriptions. As with your product's image, the majority of your customers will simply copy the descriptions provided by their suppliers. These are not easily going to help you sell your product!

Site design: Look more credible and professional than your competitors. Really really do not forjust get to simple create your essential pages, such as your return policy.

Include a video on the page for the product: Incorporating a video on your product page is another way to stand out. Not all Dropshipping companies perform this! Also, I understand that this could be time-consuming if you want to really do it for all of the products in your Drop-shipping store. Certainly if you're unfamiliar with Drop shipping and have no idea how simple things work. Therefore, I suggested focsimple using on only one to three products. These will be the initial products that you easy begin advertising. The remaining merchandise gives the impression that your store is bustling with activity and authenticity.

Account creation for your Drop shipping store

Here is something else to consider.

As previously stated, you will be launching a business, and your Drop shipping store must be viewed as such, not as a get-rich-quick scheme.

You will really need to investigate the costs associated with launching a business in your nation. For example, the cost of registering a new business.

Also, really really do not overlook the additional costs of operating a legitimate business, such as hiring a bookkeeper if you're not very good at paying your own taxes.

Chapter 20: Profitable Use Of Ppc In Your Affiliate Marketing Enterprise

Pay-Per-Click (or its popular abbreviation, PPC) is one of the four fundamental types of Search Engines. PPC is also one of the most intelligent simple method of targeted Internet advertising. According to Forbes magazine, Pay Per Click reaches 2 billion dollars annually and is projected to reach 8 billion dollars by the end of 2008.

The assumption is that you will distribute PPC advertisements on your website simple using Google AdSense.

Permit us to investigate how PPC Search Engines operate.

These engines generate listings and rank them based on a bid amount the site owner will pay for each click from that web search engine. Advertisers compete for higher placement for a particular catchphrase or expression by bidding against one another.

The highest bidder for a specific keyword or expression will have the site positioned as number one in the PPC Search Engines, followed by the second and third highest bidders, and so on, until the last number of bidders for the same keyword or expression. Your advertisements will then appear prominently on the results pages based on the amount you are willing to pay per click.

How would you generate revenue with PPC for your partner promotion business?

- Most affiliate programs pay when a sale is made or a lead is transmitted after a visitor has clicked on your site. Your revenue will be contingent on the site's content and the market's traffic volume.

The reason you should integrate PPC into your affiliate marketing program is because it is easier to generate profits than with other types of partner programs. Consequently, you will generate revenue based on the number of clicks your visitors make to the sponsor's website. Not at all like some projects, you are not compensated per transaction or activity.

PPC can be incredibly inventive for your website. With PPC Search Engines integrated into your affiliate program, you will want to capitalize on visitors who are uninspired by your products or services. Similar visitors who never return to your website.

You will not only earn commissions from people searching for products and services on the internet, but you can just also build your website's reputation as a valuable resource. Guests who have found what they were looking for on your website are likely to return and examine your offerings more thoroughly. They will ultimately return to the site to search for additional items.

This type of subsidiary program is also a straightforward way to generate additional income. For instance, when a visitor to your website performs a search in the PPC Search Engine and clicks on the publicist desired postings, the promoters' record will be deducted. You will be compensated 30% to 80% of the amount offered by the sponsors.

PPC is not just a source of simple profit; it can also help you advance your own website. Indeed, you can just use a PPC engine like Adwords to attract targeted visitors to your website.

The vast majority of initiatives permit the commissions to be spent for advertising with them quickly (not Adwords, however) and with no minimum purchase requirement. This is one of the most effective simple method for exchanging your non-targeted visitors for those who are more likely to purchase your products and services.

Chapter 21: Easily Creating A Landing Page

You must also include a captive landing page in your setup. You want to know what a landing page is.

A landing page, which is a single-page website, may contain an application form and such information about your affiliate program. The purpose of this website is to disseminate as much such information as possible while protecting the trade secrets of the program.

Before a prospective customer leaves your website, you have approximately 30 seconds to pique their interest. If you've set up this page correctly, your lead will not leave without providing their email address so you can just contact them in the future.

There are numerous websites available for this purpose. There are free alternatives such as Wix, Weebly, and LandingPages. Simply visit the site, register, and select a template to use as a starting point. Fantastically, the majority of these websites are WYSIWYG pages. You simple receive precisely what you see. Select a template and then enter the required such information simple using the affiliate program's tools.

To embed your form on your landing page, navigate back to the form you created for your mailing list and copy the HTML code. Select the widjust get to which you wish to simple add your form after pasting the HTML code into your landing page.

Save and publish your website once you've added your sign-up form and updated the content on your landing page to reflect the specifics of your affiliate program. You should record the URL for this website, as you will be marketing it to potential customers.

Chapter 22: Providing physical products and services for purchase

Although selling eBooks on websites such as JVZoo is a great way to ensure that you just keep as much money as possible, it does have a few disadvantages. Contrary to what some marketers may assert, tangible goods continue to be the most common type of online product sold.

In addition, this makes sense if you give it some serious thought. How many of your acquaintances purchase tangible goods? Almost everybody, correct? However, how many people really do you know who would purchase an eBook? If not through Kindle, your grandmother may not be able to, as she is unable to utilize PDF files. The same holds true for your friend who does not enjoy reading; they both likely would not!

As a result, you have a significantly smaller share of the market.

What steps must we just take as affiliate marketers to offer physical products? The most popular option is to become an Amazon Associate.

Amazon's associate program, which is their version of an affiliate program, attracts many marketers.

You will likely easily find that the vast majority of such information on affiliate marketing focuses on the sale of digital products via websites such as JVZoo, ClickBank, and Commission Junction.

On Amazon.com, circumstances differ. Since Amazon must pay for storage, shipping, and postage in addition to splitting profits with the manufacturer, they are typically unable to offer you a discount greater than 4 or 8 percent.

This implies that in simple order to generate a respectable profit, you will really need to sell a great deal more products at significantly higher prices.

However, must you disregard Amazon Associates as a result? In no way.

Firstly, selling physical goods is frequently considerably more profitable than selling digital goods. Which would you be more likely to spend a lot of money on: something you could hold in your hands and show to others, or something you had to read on a computer screen?

Even better, Amazon is a reputable and trustworthy brand. They can purchase from them with a single click, so they are much more likely to really do so!

Due to Amazon's vast selection of items you can just sell, there will typically be something that complements a given product.

Even if a user clicks on your URL but then purchases something else from Amazon, you will still be compensated. If you were to simple receive 8% of the sale of a new computer, for example, you could potentially earn a substantial amount of money. As long as you directed the customer to Amazon in the first place, you would simple receive the commission even if you did not actively promote the products.

The optimal solution is to employ both affiliate-marketing strategies! However, you must include Amazon in your calculations or you will suffer a loss.

To make the most of Amazon products, you will easy learn in later chapters how to market them differently.

Chapter 23: Affiliate Marketing Techniques with an Emphasis on SEO

If you want to easily increase your affiliate sales, you must easily increase your traffic-generation efforts. There are numerous simple way to accomplish this. You can just send out solo mailing ads, use pay-per-click advertising, simple create banner ads, and post in online forums, etc.

Search engine optimization may be one of the least expensive traffic generation strategies in terms of the amount of time and money required per visitor. One of the greatest benefits of SEO-generated traffic is that it continues to flow without additional effort or expense.

Having said that, you are likely familiar with the numerous common simple method for generating traffic. You are familiar with utilizing tags, implementing keyword optimization, submitting articles to directories, acquiring backlinks, etc. Nothing novel here. You've attempted these simple method and either obtained results or not).

At this point, you'll want to easily find a pair of feathers to simple add to your cap – a handful of truly unique SEO techniques that you can just use to such improve your results. Affiliate marketing offers a variety of intriguing options.

Through search engine optimization, you can just generate traffic for little or no cost simple using a variety of strategies. For example, you may simple create a forum on your website and encourage users to participate. This would not only enable you to encourage duplicate traffic, but it would also enable your visitors to generate quantity, which search engines would rank and associate with your website.

You can just purchase or simple create scripts that automatically collect and display unique product information.

Google will just take note of this the next time they evaluate your website, and your search engine ranking positions are likely to change as a result.

When it comes down to it, you have numerous options for improving your search engine ranking positions, and doing so is frequently less expensive than simple using pay-per-click traffic sources. Include some of the aforementioned strategies in your arsenal and employ them to generate traffic.

Chapter 24: Combining Google Ad Sense And Affiliate Marketing Maximizes Profits

You manage a website and require funds to just keep it online. Can you survive solely on your website, or really do you have other sources of income? Affiliate marketing may be useful for both webmasters and publishers if they require financial assistance. Affiliate marketing has the potential to generate rapid wealth. Why not also join the Google Adsense program if your website contains a wealth of valuable content and you wish to easily increase your revenue?

What purpose does affiliate marketing serve?

Unless you are a business owner who prefers to sell his or her own products online rather than promote those of others, affiliate marketing is the best and easiest way to make money online. Affiliate marketing is advantageous not only for affiliates but also for merchants who operate online stores. In an affiliate marketing arrangement, one website functions as the merchant and the other as the affiliate. Affiliate has agreed to host Merchant's product advertisements on its website. Regarding payment, the merchant would use the affiliate's preferred method of receiving funds. The affiliate really need only host the retailer's advertisement on his site to easy begin earning commission. This arrangement would also greatly benefit the merchant, as paying affiliates to market their products is significantly less expensive than paying an advertising agency to really do the same. Depending on the retailer, the affiliate may be compensated in a variety of ways, and the webmaster can use this such information to his advantage. The pay-per-click model, the pay-per-lead model, and the pay-per-sale model are common simple method by which online marketers are compensated. Affiliates enjoy the pay-per-click model because it only requires a visit to the advertiser's website for them to generate revenue. However, merchants prefer the latter two options because they only pay you if your visitor subscribes to their service or makes a purchase.

However, the number of visitors your website receives is more important than how affiliates are compensated in determining whether or not an affiliate marketing program generates a profit. Affiliate marketing strategies typically yield greater returns for websites with more visitors.

What about Google's Adsense?

Google Adsense may be thought of as an affiliate program to some extent. With

Google Adsense, Google acts as an intermediary between affiliates and businesses. In this scenario, the retailer would register with Google and feed the search engine company text advertisements pertaining to the products they sell. These advertisements, which are merely links to the advertiser's website, would then appear in Google search results and on the websites of affiliates or webmasters who are members of the Google Adsense program. There are many similarities between Google Adsense and other affiliate marketing programs, but there are also significant differences. With Google Adsense, a website owner really need only include a small amount of code on his website, and Google will handle the rest. The advertisements displayed on your website would be contextually relevant. This would benefit both you and the advertiser, as visitors to your website would be more likely to be interested in the products being offered. Affiliates simple receive a commission based on the number of clicks their Google Adsense advertisements receive. Google would send you a check for the amount advertisers pay per click on an ad displayed on your website, after deducting their fee. Google Adsense typically sends out payments once per month. In addition, Google Adsense simply provides webmasters with a tracking tool that displays such information about the amount of money earned from each advertisement.

Where really do these hints ultimately lead us?

Clearly, nowhere else besides the bank! Simple using affiliate marketing and the Google Adsense program is beneficial for both merchants and affiliates. Affiliate marketing can save merchants substantial sums of money when compared to working with advertising agencies. You can just make a lot of money as a webmaster by doing what you're good at: easily Creating websites. If you combine Google Adsense with other affiliate marketing networks, you have the potential to earn a significant amount of money.

www.ingramcontent.com/pod-product-compliance
Lightning Source LLC
LaVergne TN
LVHW011718060526
838200LV00051B/2948